Beginning With Your Last Breath

Beginning With Your Last Breath

Roy McFarlane

Nine
Arches
Press

Beginning With Your Last Breath
Roy McFarlane

ISBN: 978-1-911027-08-9

First published September 2016 by:

Nine Arches Press
PO Box 6269
Rugby
CV21 9NL
United Kingdom
www.ninearchespress.com

Printed in Britain by:
The Russell Press Ltd.

Nine Arches Press is supported using public funding by the National Lottery through Arts Council England.

Supported using public funding by
ARTS COUNCIL ENGLAND

To Percella Araisa McFarlane
an extraordinary and beautiful mother

Contents

I

'The word for love, habib, is written from right
to left, starting where we would end it
and ending where we might begin.'

'A Soldier's Arabic' – Brian Turner

Papers

The day I was called into my mother's bedroom
the smell of cornmeal porridge still coloured the air,

windowsills full of plants bloomed
and dresses half-done hung from wardrobe doors

and her Singer sewing machine came to rest
like a mail train arriving at its final destination,

foot off the pedal, radio turned down, she beckoned,
touched me with those loving hands.

Shrouded in the softness of light from the net curtains,
her eyes filled with sensitivity, hesitated as she spoke to me,

sit down son, there's something I need to tell you.

She picked up her heavy Bible with gold-edged leaves,
turning the pages as they whispered and somewhere

in the middle of Psalms she removed a sheet of paper
which read, *'In the matter of the Adoption Act. 1958'*

and I'm lost in the reading of a name of an infant,
sinking in to the cream background, falling between the lines.

Only the tenderness of her voice drew me out of the margins;
words fallen now echo through the years.

We adopted you from the age of 6 months,

enveloped by this revelation I couldn't move,
imagined it couldn't be right because I knew my mother;

the aroma of her Morgan pomaded hair, her olive oiled skin,
the Y scarred throat that she hid under buttoned up blouses,

and like a hymn I found myself telling her, *it's alright, it's alright.*

The weight of knowing

The woman in the photograph
surrounded by siblings looking just like me;
this was the woman who gave me away.

And now she wanted to know me,
trying to connect to me. Unbelievable, coming from
the woman in the photograph.

It was my turn to reject, stuff my emotions away,
ready to make a quick getaway because
this was the woman who gave me away.

The weight of knowing her was too heavy to put on,
and my anger tipped the scales beyond reason.
The woman in the photograph

sent me letters to leave me in a spell
but I was conjured by memories that
this was the woman who gave me away.

And those eyes telling their tales
and untold stories couldn't change the fact of
the woman in the photograph;
this was the woman who gave me away.

Painting

She ain't holding them up; she's holding on
(some English Rose) by Sonia Boyce, 1986

I saw my mother in this painting of Sonia Boyce;
the woman wearing a cerise dress with black roses,
holding her family above her head – a basket of life.
And like her she was holding us up,
her load no lighter for having two babies
out of wedlock, holding on, making a life
in strange places, fighting the struggle of womanhood.

Love evaded her twice, men she couldn't hold on to,
no matter how wide she opened her heart.
Holding on to any job whilst handing over her babies
to be held by others until she returned, tired and weary.
Holding on to hope that a childless couple would take
care of the one she'd leave behind; knowing
that her last breath upon his skin would be a new beginning.

Fragments of a mother and son story

I surrendered unto the unknown,
followed the route my mother took
and looked out the window and wondered if she
thought of what she left behind
or flew into the future blindly
towards some distant star
that migrant birds are guided by.
From London to Toronto to Winnipeg,
a day of travelling to find meaning to
my years of roaming; flying back in time
to a place eight hours behind
to find the beginning of my journey.

*

I land in the evening with all that I have;
a stomach filled with caged birds and despair,
thinking what the hell I was doing there.
A stranger greets me:
You must be Jenny's son,
and I cry within to be called somebody's child.
She smiles, coos with excitement,
oh my God, you look so much like her.
I forget everything; the birds settle within.
She's like a magpie, this friend of my mother,
hoarding the fragility of my being
trying to put together
the fragments of a mother and son story.

*

We're driving through districts
where neon lights glow above shop windows,
where people drive on the wrong side of the road,
where traffic lights hang high in the sky.
We're driving for miles across a flattened sepia scene,
no hills no valleys no nothing, flat as the eyes can see.
We're driving into a neighbourhood
where streets are wider than football pitches
where drivers are polite to each other
where everywhere is green, quiet and clean
and the only noise is the humming of the air conditioner
and this woman's continued cooing, *I can't wait to see
    Jenny's face.*

*

We arrive and we're told to go in the basement;
in England they're cold dark damp places,
in Winnipeg they're another world
with a bar, drinks cabinet, pool table, sofas, a large TV.
She's here, our host announces, fluttering around us
and the birds' wings beat against the bars again.
They close the door.
I hear her voice and I start to cry.
I hear her footsteps, so beautiful, so light.
The door opens and I see her silhouette
I see her walk down the stairs,
I see her and she sees me.
She cries out,
My son, my son.

My mother, sister and I return to the place where I was born

Beginning at
North Street,
memories condemned
speak through aged houses,
tall, confined, conspiring
clandestine in their closeness.
Peeling paint-work, boarded windows.
They still live between alleyways;
rumours and gossips and tall tales
that drove her away, memories
that speak into my mother's ears.

Ending at
Handsworth Road,
tree-lined streets whisper of our arrival.
Houses paired up, lean into each other
knowingly watching us,
observing our every move as
we walk along wider roads
my elder sister rubs past walls
releasing forbidden genies
and she shudders as it all rushes back
and she wishes to go home as mother stands
listening to the past murmured on the wind.

II

'A light song of light is not sung in the light; what would be the point? ...but saves its full voice for midnight.'

'Twelve Notes for A Light Song of Light'
– Kei Miller

That place just off the M6

Out of the darkness cometh light
Coat of Arms of the Wolverhampton City Council

I've always wondered why Black people
came to Wolverhampton,
that place just off the M6
in the middle of nowhere.

Queen Victoria called it the Black Country.
Black Country! Black people!
Where else would they go?

It's the place of the *yam, yam*.
Well, Black people nyam yam,
sweet potatoes and tings.

Yow spake funny, *yam bostin*.
They felt at home with people
who couldn't speak the Queen's English.

The black and gold of the Wolves
like myths of streets paved with gold drawing
Blacks and Asians from across the world to Waterloo Road.

So why Enoch? Why speak of forebode?
River Tiber foaming with much blood
when blood had already been spilt in the name of nationality.

And look at the bronze Lady Wulfruna
like the statue of liberty
welcoming the poor and the needy;

instead they were welcomed with closed doors,
cold looks and biting words
in a bitter climate.

I've always wondered why Black people
came to Wolverhampton,
that place just of the M6
in the middle of nowhere.

The *black corner* of Wolverhampton

House-sitting for my godfather on the 9th floor
of Blakenhall flats, the *black corner* of Wolverhampton,
a world where I looked out to far horizons;
reached beyond glass panes, touched the whites of the skies.

A world all to myself when he went to work,
into the cool of the night, warning me
with his Sammy Davis Jr smile not to put on
his snakeskin shoes as he closed the door behind him.

A world to myself with the TV on through the night
watching Richard Pryor live, swallowed up
in a retro black swivel armchair until
Earth, Wind and Fire transported me to boogie wonderland.

A world where you could see smoke rise from chimneys
and if you blinked you'd swear that you saw someone fall.
Where nights rode the back of velvet-coloured skies
and vertigo was more than a Hitchcock movie.

A world where I voyaged to the bottom of the sea
in command of the Seaview; I was a black Spy
for the men from U.N.C.L.E; kissed Lieutenant Uhru
on the SS Enterprise and fell back to earth.

A world where I put on my polo neck,
rolled up my sleeve and bounced with attitude,
I was Shaft, bad motherfucker, diving over sofas,
moving from room to room with a cocked finger.

A world where *Hustler* fell out of turned-over sofas;
turning page after page of exposed flesh,
centrefolds wide open; eyes devoured forbidden fruits
before a gallery of him and Christ looking down on me.

A world where people actually flew out of nightmares
and Guardian angels didn't fly just in time to prevent
the graffiti of pavements and walls with
the ending of people's hopes and dreams.

A world which came to an end the night my godfather
threw me out, returning early to Marvin Gaye
playing love songs and me squeezing the life out
of his snakeskin shoes with my size tens.

In Memory of Boxing

How does Mike Tyson measure up to all those greats?
Only dad and myself would be thinking of those things,
as Tyson prowled around the rigid Frank Bruno
waiting for the bell to release the beast within.
My dad's in his favourite armchair in front of the TV,
fighting the tiredness that circles him,
eyes closing, he's turning the dial back on time.

He's a young man working his father's farm
under the bruising heat of a Caribbean sun,
and when the sun lets up, he's with his father and others
gathered around a radio player, listening in black and white
to the fight of Joe Louis and Max Schmeling. And he's hurting,
because the chance to go to America has gone, to work the farms
where young black men are warned not to look on white women.

The bell clanged, Schmeling's down three times already,
the Brown Bomber throwing rib-cracking, body-punishing blows
and like Langston Hughes said, never before has one man
brought a sense of black pride across the air waves;
he's deep in sleep now, turning the dial on a large TV,
where a son gets to stay up late
to watch the *Rumble in the Jungle*.

He's middle-aged, labouring in the ring of the steel industry
caught up in the cold of the British Isles,
taken the best that life could throw at him
leaving him battered and bruised, hanging on the ropes;
eight rounds later Ali's coming off the ropes,
Ali's throwing a punch, Foreman's spinning, he's spiralling,
he's fallen and Ali declares to the world, *I am the greatest*.

In the present I've turned the volume down
and Bruno, the pride of a nation, is holding on
like a wildebeest caught on a muddy bank;
Tyson staggers him and moves in for the kill.
And the question of how Tyson compares to all those greats
seems so long ago, just as the referee saves Bruno from a mauling,
and my father smiles in his sleep, turning the dial on his memories.

Baptism

Rastaman John the Baptist
baptised a young man name Jesus.
A voice in the wilderness calling
revolutionary friends to step right in

rather than stand at the edge;
and I wonder if John saw the vexation
of upturned tables, if he saw those missed years
of Christ that are not canonised.

I wonder if he saw me and Bevan
getting baptised like a rite of passage
in a sacred place, our families,
friends and those we knew

stood around a hole
they cut out of the ground;
a baptismal pool for dipping sinners
who cried, confessed and raised up sinless.

I wonder if he saw Jackie and Marie
dressed in white go under,
rise out of the waters; their bodies like Venus
dancing before us, looking back at us,

wet blouses clinging, skirts sticking;
we nearly lost our heads whilst elderly sisters
rushed to veil their decency with
outstretched arms and bath towels.

And did Rastaman John the Baptist
foresee his death, head on a platter, because
of all those who watched Salome dance –
men baptised in a sea of sensuality.

Night and Day

I learned verses of love with
a beautiful two-tone Rudie,
her tight jeans and t-shirts held
her as intimately as I did in the day time
in between lessons, common room
and the sports hall. We kissed like
lovers from a Klimt painting; our bodies
ablaze with the touch of each other
and we made love in open fields
painting beautiful colours
until the sun went down...
          night times
we sneaked out; the daughter
of a single mother and the son
of a preacher man; star-crossed lovers
at the Rising Star or The Molineux
waiting for the healing of Lover's Rock
where bass speakers mesmerised,
locked us together in perfect poetry,
the symmetry of a Rodin sculpture
brought to life on the dance floor,
lost in Janet Kaye's *Silly Games*.

Patterson's House

Patterson was the old man of the neighbourhood
that young men drowning in oceans of puberty,
navigating skies of spirituality,
and living in times of uncertainty,
found in him a lighthouse for all seasons.

We brought our baggage, basketballs and bicycles
into the hall, laid our keys and bus passes
on a table that took the weight of our anger,
groaned under the guilt of sexual awakening
and was big enough for the vast canvass of blackness.

We had the freedom of his house,
to walk into rooms filled with stories
of how he lied about his age to join the Air Force
to be stationed in England, and after the war
loved and danced all night under Cuban sunsets,

to leave on the dawn of revolutions.
And ending up back in England
to start a new life in Smethwick,
meeting Malcolm X on Marshall Street –
nine days before they shot him in Harlem.

Weekends were the best;
a pot of soup on Saturdays that never ran out,
filled with answers, love and understanding.
And on Sundays, chicken, rice and peas
and rivers flowing with Guinness punch.

The light never went out at Patterson's:
a place that felt like Beulah land,
where heaven didn't feel so far away
and being a teenager didn't feel like a cross
on our backs, carried through fields of guilt.

Saturday Soup

Bevan is smiling into his soup, juggling with
the choice of dumpling or dasheen to devour,
Do you think things will ever get better for us?
I'm hugging the bowl my mother places before me
the smell draws me in. The swirling, twirling
wisp of heat that snakes into the air hypnotizes me.
He breaks the trance and continues, *I'm sick and tired*
of all of this – pointing to the colour of his skin –
I'm tired of fighting and fitting in.
I'm sucking on a bone and find a response
amongst the sweet potatoes and cho-cho.
War is not the answer, only love can conquer hate.
He laughed, we chewed on other thoughts
and let Marvin Gaye tell us *What's Going On.*

I was writing city lyrics,
the poetics of the oppressed,
Bevan was an Urban Rembrandt
drawing revolutions of the young.
He was six-feet wound-up length of muscle
often times we'd wrestle and play-
fight until bruises mushroomed leaving
fallouts that blew away friendship
for that split second, barely standing
until rescued by the bonds of laughter.
We were brothers not by blood, but by the
late evenings where we sat in front of electric fires,
told stories to the dawn of the new morning
and wore out the tape of *Enter the Dragon.*

The Tebbit Test (Patriotism)

The Tebbit test, that litmus test of Britishness:
dip us deep enough and we should come out
red, white and blue, but we wore the
colours of Jamaica when the West Indies
cricket team black-washed England or turned
to the *Reggae Boyz* for the faintest of hopes of victory
when they reached the World Cup Final.

Long before the Tebbit test, we – Young Black
British – had been plunged in the cauldron
of brutishness and found no black in the Union Jack,
except for those Olympic occasions where
Daley Thompson, Tessa Sanderson and
Linford Christie wrapped themselves in the Union flag –
a hiatus from the hate, a jubilee for all things sable.

Yet Blacks and Asians we're more used
to the engulfing experience of John Barnes,
the genius, the wizard that scored against Brazil,
cutting through their defence with pure beauty.
Only to be reminded a few days later on a plane
returning home, filled with the England team and supporters,
that goal don't count, the one scored by the nigger.

After all is said and done

After a summer of loving and late nightclubbing
after we danced all night with our sweet lovers
after we separated to go our different ways –
a bunch of skinheads were watching Bevan
walking alone, walking with his thoughts
of love and the beauty of a sole star
etching its story across the darkness.

Now Bevan's running through shopping avenues where street lights
shine off his sweating forehead and the heat of his body
leaves a signature in the cool air, whilst mannequins standstill,
watching dumbfounded the deadly chase in a city gone to sleep.
Bevan's running through St Peter's Gardens where fountains dry
can't quench the deadly thirst of rampant, raging hate
and cherubim with empty gestures observe his every move
and Christ, well Christ looks down helplessly, nailed to his cross.

Bevan's running past silhouettes in the Cimmerian shade of night
Bevan's running past naked trees looking down on his plight
Bevan's running past closed doors behind black gates
Bevan's running past a headless Anglo-Saxon cross.
And church walls are void of saints and angels,
stark in the colour of the moonlight
whilst stained glass windows withhold their splendour
as he's running down church steps past Lady Wulfruna.

After all that running, Bevan's tired of holding it in
and standing in the circle of hostility, he makes a stand.
After head butts, broken nose, fist flying with black pride,
he's down, broken, beaten and bleeding in St Peter's Square.
After morning prayers and Sunday preaching,
he still believed, but stopped calling on Jesus.
After he lived the life, paid the price, he opens up his sketchbook
and captures the whole world in the eyes of those behind bars.

Surrender to the air

'You wanna fly, you got to give up the shit that weighs you down.'
'If you surrendered to the air, you could ride it.'
from *Song of Solomon* –Toni Morrison

Wherever there was a court we played:
one-on-one, inside, outside
night or day, sunshine or rain.
We played hard, leaned heavy,
shoulder into opponent's chest,
guarding space and ball with body,
One arm outstretched to shield
the bounce of the ball,
no give or take.

That's how we played,
tussled and wrestled,
slapped the ball
    if it suspended in the air long enough.

Through the legs,
round the back,
fake the drive,
spin the other way.

    Then there was the opening:
    the chance we should always take
    the gap that opens,

driving to the board like Pegasus
we'd invoke the lay-up sequence.

1st stride,
    2nd stride,

and the launch into the air
defying gravity

our wings outstretched.

We glided knowing that we were beauty in motion,
bodies elite, that when we released

that ball
after the double-pump...

we had surrendered to the air.

for Bevan

Burning with a rage that Babylon would never understand...

Just de police and dem stupidity
And dem keeping up on black people
Handsworth Songs: Dir John Akomfarh

We watched Handsworth burning
from the top of the hill
after the spreading of words
like wildfire through
gyms, common rooms
and on the streets.
Wi gwan burn down the place.
Babylon gwan burn down tonight.

Bring me my Bow of burning gold

Words alight on tongues;
unlike Nero we had no power
only the fire in our belly
ignited by the lies, the daily abuse,
state sanctioned terror
of a Sus law that was
beating us down.

Unemployed and unwanted
living in Maggie's world,
where there was no such thing
as society; she played her fiddle
and we played our song
all night long.

Bring me my Arrows of desire

The 'torch of hate'
was injustice and anger mixed
in a Molotov cocktail thrown
at the terrorists of the state,
their shields hopeless
as we were, under
the daily onslaught of racism.

Nero blamed Christians, Maggie's media
blamed Rastafarians who flashed their locks
silhouetted against the backdrop
of burning streets, blazing golden red
in a halo of smoke.

Bring me my Spear: O clouds unfold!

Anarchy was everybody's cloak
Blacks, Asians and Whites caught up
in the winter of Maggie's policies,
standing on the streets watching
firemen trying to put out flames,
chanting *let it burn, let it burn.*

*'Would to God that all
the Lord's people were Prophets.'*
And saw what we saw on the hills of
Handsworth, Brixton, Toxteth
and Broadwater Farm as they burned
in a whirlwind of fire.

Bring me my Chariot of fire!

Saving our Sons

*Blacks, Asians, Whites, we all live in the same community,
why do we have to kill one another… I lost my son, step
forward if you want to lose your son.*
Tariq Jahan, Father of Haroon Jahan, killed in the
Birmingham riots, August 2011

A father's hands are red;
he's trying like a midwife
to keep him alive in the cradle of his arms.

The heat of his body,
the warmth of his breath
ebbing away in the midst of rioting,

the chaos and destruction
dark abyss of madness
drawn from the womb of our city.

There's vengeance and violence
swiftly swelling and poisoning
the blood that flows through young minds.

Hours later, the father who has lost his son
needs an antidote for the growing toxicity;
he refuses to lose another and with

outstretched hands pleading to a crowd
for the insanity to stop; he cries
for the re-birth of hope that will save our sons.

Finding *X/Self*

after Edward Kamau Brathwaite

Many years ago   a resource centre was throwing away
literature from the widest four corners of the
African diaspora   a sea of books   to sail   to make
a voyage of discovery of New Words

Edward Kamau Brathwaite *X/Self*
finds me

-1 MAR 1999
40p
X/SELF
Withdrawn

The words that follow   I never fully understand
but page after page are turned greedily
eyes become fat and mouth become full
with verse and lyrics that leave their sweet taste:

'towards
My heart at wounded knee'

'towards
Red Tacky bleeding in the West'

Something sings a litany to me
fills my angry African self with belief
weighs heavy on my birthright

spins my triangle back to its beginning
gives me back my obelisk
                    Creating my own narrative

towards
James Cone liberating Black Theology

towards
Malcolm writing from Mecca

towards
Small axe   big tree Bob Marley

towards
Martin Luther King's dreams in a living nightmare

To the voice that walk across blared lines of humanity
a narrative free of constraints
                self so assured it lives
beyond the boundaries dictated

towards
Nanny of the maroons catching bullets with her bottom

towards
The bare foot fakir/ Gandhi that brought the British Empire
        down

towards
A God/Allah/Jehovah without a name to fight or kill for

towards
Marvin Gaye and God save the children

III

'*If the spirit moves you*
Let me groove you good'

'Let's Get It On' – Marvin Gaye

A Love Supreme

Musical Setting by Steve Tromans

She was holding the album of
'A Love Supreme' as if she was carrying the Word
stroking and caressing the cover
as if they were lovers and I   just an observer

We were the sons and daughters of jazz
in a world of Michael Jackson and Bob Marley
seeing things in the colour of hip-hop reggae and R&B
she drew me into her inner-circle

Home alone in her mother's front room
she withdrew the black vinyl from its sleeve
and laid it tenderly on a revolving wheel
dropping the needle into a willing and expectant groove

> *Piano/percussion play opening to A Love Supreme*
> *then start the bassline pattern*

A love supreme
quiet and unrestrained
as walking by a summer stream
or shading under a tree
watching sunlight sprinkle through

whilst hearing the footsteps of melody
over an enchanting rhapsody

A Love Supreme
   A Love Supreme
      A Love Supreme
         A Love Supreme

These were the evenings of summer loving
drinking from each other in the cool of the evening
she showed me the sacred as we lay there naked
in the mantra of love   ready to break bread and drink wine

We set ourselves free and lost ourselves
in spiritual overtures baptised over and over in fire
in the passion of love   we knew each other for the first time
speaking tongues of sensuality and trembling in each other's arms

In the stillness something sacred had been created
and we were translated to an upper room
maybe 42nd street   maybe the Vanguard
where we watched the gathering around the table

Monk sitting bowing his head
stomping his feet   tapping his fingers
whilst away from the table in his pork-pie hat
Lester's looking out the window
for some long lost melody or waiting for Lady Day
because you know they don't talk no more

Piano plays darker-toned harmonies

And Miles with his head bandaged and his jacket blood-stained
he's vexed   burning with rage long before the police
beat him bloody with a billy club for being black
long before veins were full of anger   long before
the intravenous drip of drugs and sex that never calmed him

Piano plays lighter-colour harmonies

Dizzy's laughing eyes wide open   cheeks bloated
clowning around   trying to lighten the moment

Salt peanuts   salt peanuts   where's the salt peanuts
but Miles is not feeling it and Dizzy's losing it
and then we hear that beautiful melody

A Love Supreme
   A Love Supreme
      A Love Supreme
         A Love Supreme

         Piano and Perc change to a new harmonic pattern

Art Blakey can't understand the fussing and fighting
Fire is what they want   fire that washes the dust of everyday life

Dexter Gordon's looking cool   dressed to the nines
he's already done time and now he's running
running all the way to Paris
where he can play music to those
who listen with ears and not with their eyes

Chet Baker he's keeping cool   keeping quiet   keeping time
in his own mind   keeping out the way of Miles
since the *New York Times* made him the greatest trumpet player
Chet keeping quiet   keeping time

And Monk's walking   dancing in a trance because he can hear

A Love Supreme
   A Love Supreme
      A Love Supreme
         A Love Supreme

         Piano plays darker harmonies

Mingus and Miles are brewing up a storm
Miles won't take no shit no more   won't be called

nigger no more and Mingus he's making fables
making bass lines that will change minds

And Bird has just walked in   late   lost and out of it
dishevelled with the devil on his back and in his veins

Young Clifford Brown blowing a horn
like midnight was around the corner
like time was going
to turn Judas on all of their ass

And John takes giant steps into the room
like they've all been waiting
made his presence known
because John had been to Gethsemane and back
saw what was on the horizon   for you and me
and all we need is

A Love Supreme
    A Love Supreme
        A Love Supreme
            A Love Supreme

            Piano and Perc change to Slow, Free tempo

The greatest gift we have is *A Love Supreme*
whether it's two lovers wrapped around each other
or a world determined to be betrayed by hate
together we can break the bread and drink the cup of

A Love Supreme
    A Love Supreme
        A Love Supreme
            A Love Supreme

                Piano plays rising chords till end

I found my father's love letters

To my unknown father

I found my father's love letters
in strange and obscure places,
hidden in dark secret spaces,
where memories had closed the doors.

I found blank letters, with matching cards and envelopes.
A small drawer filled with letters unfinished,
crossed through, curling at the edges,
turning in the colour of time.

There was one in Marquez's *Love in the Time of Cholera*
sandwiched somewhere between
Fermina's rejection of Floretina
and a lifetime of loving, waiting for true love.

I found some penned in a note pad, half-written, half-thought,
scribbled to capture fleeting thoughts,
earnest in writing the emotional overflow
that time edits into streams flowing over with love.

I found one folded
lost in the attic
an elegy to love
that time had forgotten.

I searched to find the true name to those letters entitled *my love*.
A secret lover? Distant lover? First time lover?
or even my mother of whom you gave a thousand names
but I never heard you call her *my love*.

Lost in Birmingham

… do not arouse or awaken love until it so desires. **Song of Solomon 3:5**

She lives in the Electric theatre where once we watched Chico & Rita,
in sofas deep enough to hold on to dreams and desires.

She's in the Edwardian Tea Rooms sharing Earl Grey
and Cornish clotted cream scones on a summer afternoon.

She's walking around the Rotunda along New Street listening
to the moan of love from a saxophone in the hands of a street busker.

She's Andromeda waiting for Perseus
to release her from the halls of the Museum and Art Gallery.

She's swallowed up in the silver whale of Selfridges;
entangled in the enchantment, consumed by her desires.

She's speaking in tongues or saying confessions,
a wandering soul searching to be whole.

She's homeless but believes, holding on to sweet memories.
A love that should never have been stirred until the time was ready.

The beauty of a scar

There was a mark across the skies
over Sedgley Beacon, sun seeping
through a blood shot-horizon,
the faintest of clouds left
a blemish across the skies.

Similar to the one that lies
upon your chest,
floating above your breast,
spreading along the line of your clavicle,
a wisp, a whirl that snakes up your neck
and hides conveniently under your
flowing raven hair.

A scar that glows crimson
in the midst of our love making,
touched and kissed
a thousand times
I know its texture
ingrained across my mind
your beautiful skin next to mine.

And you've learned to love it
never to hide it, on display for all to see
as if God had touched you especially
like the mark he left across the skies
over Sedgley Beacon.

The day after we argued

I'm away from you in Chester after a night's
performance at Alexander's, and I'm walking by
a river filled with the abundance of rain;
two swans a distance apart
with necks curved back and wings aroused,
half raised, sailed slowly towards each other.

Viewing from a bridge with a friend,
she whispered *you can never tell if they're*
defending their area or if they're lovers;
but these mirrored question marks met

together making a love heart.
Wings settled, caressing each other's neck,
stroking each other's body, beaks pushing
between the folds of willing wings.

Never say goodbye

In the middle of *Kabhi Alvida Naa Kehna*
I told you it always rains in Bollywood movies
you laughed; pressed yourself against me
under the glow of blue rain from the screen.

That was last night, now
we're damp in the morning dew of loving
that covers our whole body, gentle in lightness.

The dew leaves droplets of sensuality in every space
that can be named and others that can't,
requiring mouths and hands to christen our desire.

And without us noticing it begins to rain;
tentative drops that appear on a window pane,
drops that draw lines of rivulets, tongue trailing
across my chest and down my abdomen.

And we get caught out in the rain, wet,
we grab a hold of body and mind, slip and slide,
into streams flowing with the music of our lovemaking.

So how can you say we should never be together
when we're adrift in lakes reflecting our love
floating to where we'll never say goodbye?

As I did the night before

It was the way you used to put your tights on,
after a moment of loving
    or at the dawn of a new morning.
There was nothing more sensual
    or visual than you sitting at the edge of the bed
taking your tights in your hands;
softly, tenderly lost in that moment of intimacy.

And you'd begin
with one leg folded into your body,
your foot pointed elegantly
unrolling a film of nylon
that would sheath and cling
over tips of toes,
ball and sole,
arch and ankle,
over stubborn heel,
sailing steadily
up the calf of an extended leg.
A ritual so beautiful
it had to be repeated.

And when completed,
with both feet on the ground
you would rise,
gracefully poised as a ballerina
at the *barre*,
    bending at the waist with legs straight
you would unroll the rest of your garment
with sweet dexterity
across knees and up golden thighs

until they finally ascended
over a round delicate derrière
where waist bands settle
and the gusset reaches the meeting of your thighs.

And you stood tiptoe,
body stretched and arched for a moment.
You held that pose.

Finally with an encore
you bend over one more time
caressing and smoothing out
folds or ripples that you find
    as I did the night before
when we had reached our pinnacle
I held you tenderly and lovingly
eased out the swell and tide
that still lingered in the bodies
of two lovers overwhelmed in love.

The Baroness and the Monk

Pannonica de Koenigswater & Thelonious Monk

They told her about the Monk
But she had to find out for herself
Listened twenty times

To the sounds of 'Round Midnight'

Never heard
Anything so sublime
Bewitched entranced

> *Time eluded her*

Seduced and slayed

> *She missed her flight*

Left her husband behind
Abandoned all her children

> *Just to follow*

A poet in Amsterdam

They never told me about a city
alive with living breathing bicycles
there's bikes, bikes everywhere.
They're leaning against railings and walls
tied to landmarks and lampposts
hiding under bridges and stairwells
loitering in alleyways and backstreets
standing outside shops and cafes
there's bikes, bikes everywhere.
They travel on boats across waterways
they glide by you and frighten you
sneak up to you and scare you
jump out of shadows behind you
there's bikes, bikes everywhere.
They're the social constructors of Amsterdam
they're modern day cupids they don't give a damn
they entice you into your first kiss
making you stutter and utter
can I walk you to your bike?
And before you know it you're asking
can we lock our bikes together?
And now you're riding on a bicycle made for two
and seven years later
you got babies, babies in the front
babies in the back, babies in seats
and carriers on your shoulder
there's bikes, bikes everywhere.
Don't you see it, don't you understand it
there's bike city with bikes stacked sky high
on top of each other
next to each other

those brazen bikes are doing it day and night
and when I'm trying to go to sleep
I'm counting bikes instead of sheep
there's bikes, bikes everywhere.

Tipton

Tipton, this tongue-tipping
double syllable of a word,
this Bermuda Triangle
between Brum and Wolves.
This *lost city* quintessentially
Black Country, God's belly button
of the Universe has got me.

I'm 10 and visiting the cousins,
the only black family in Princess Ends.
Streets wide enough to pass on gossip
and a horse in somebody's front garden.

I watched cousins as dark as the *cut,*
larger than life, colourful as the Caribbean,
speak another language.
Only laughter, sweets and pots of soup
translated us back to a common understanding.

Ow's ower kid their father would say
with vowels big and round as his obese body,
then he'd give me a sweet, slap me on my back
and laugh his way into the kitchen.
I asked my cousin *what did he say?*
Yam saft, she'd say gurgling,
everybody laughing like the locks at the back,
where water poured in and everybody rises,
whether you wanted or not,
a lock that levelled off once the father
left to go to the pub or to the steelworks.

40 years later I'm back
walking past the pie factory where they serve
soul nights on sawdust covered floors.

Industries put to an eternal sleep
turning into a commuter town, it
still draws on you, pulls on you.
Yam olright it's dem lot
that are causing de problems,
with syllables that jab and slash,
sentences like the Tipton Slasher
the bare knuckle verbosity of it.
And there's an *oss* everywhere,
in somebody's garden, along the street
and a metal *oss* frozen in time
by the railway station
and an anchor
on the side of the road.
Not all things are anchored
in time or in a living museum;
cultures flow, merge and make
their own journeys into front rooms
as I say to me *bab* bending over
I cor walk past ya without
putting me onds on ya and I know that

Tipton, this tongue-tipping
double syllable of a word,
this Bermuda Triangle
between Brum and Wolves.
This *lost city* quintessentially
Black Country, God's belly button
of the Universe has got me.

Nearly There (I)

Nina

Do you remember the day we got caught
in a torrential down pour?
We'd just stepped off the bus
on a summer's day and we had to make
a decision to stay under cover
or run the gauntlet of the rain.

We ran.
I urged, pulled and dragged you along
watched those little legs scurry along
and kept on telling you
we're nearly there.
I'm your father, what else could I say?

So,
I covered you in my bomber jacket
under a shower of rain
as the windows of heaven opened,
turning roads into rivers
and junctions into waterways;

we walked on water
waded deep in ravines
and in the deluge of it all
I was overwhelmed with tears
as I kept on telling you
we're nearly there.

And when we were finally there
we got rid of our wet clothes,
wrapped you up in love
made you *chocolate-tea*
and sat you down
in front of a warm fire.

I won't always be there
when it pours – and it will pour –
to drag you through the rain,
to carry you along the way
but remember, when it rains,
you're nearly there.

IV

The wound is the place where the light enters you.

Rumi

The year Maya Angelou died

In the year that Maya Angelou died
she appeared to me in a dream and I cried.

She was as real as the words on this page; caressed
all my fears with the healing touch of lightness,

finding depths and places
that I'd never been and left traces

of her love and tenderness,
illuminating paths edged with gentleness

taking me to rainbows that are
formed in the rains of despair.

And somewhere there I found my mother
waiting for me to wipe away my tears

where words fat and ripe fell off mango trees
and Mayflies lived for an eternity.

Lighting up History

*"I trust that England will not forget one who nursed the sick, who
sought out her wounded to aid and succor them, and who performed
the last offices for some of her illustrious dead."*
Sir William Howard Russell, War Correspondent, *The Times,* 1857.

'In which war was Mary Seacole made famous for nursing
on the battlefield:
    World War 1
    Crimean War
    Boer War'

She chooses the wrong answer – a TV game show contestant –
I tut and turn to the notes on my iPhone when the woman
next to me, previously marking multiple-choice questions

shakes her head and speaks my mind.
It's terrible that we don't recognise what she's done, she draws closer
I hate it when they call her the black Florence Nightingale.

Our conversation lights up the radiology ward, as she's on fire
this trainer of nurses, who wants more recognition
for this gallant and brave lady, unlike

Michael Gove and the *Daily Mail*: the former desires
to remove her from the curriculum, the latter bringing her
into disrepute, calling her the making of a PC myth.

I wait for my mother and she waits for her husband
and we wait for a society to bring to light *herstory*
and we trust that England will not let her memory die.

Leaves are falling

I didn't notice the leaves falling
the day they told me it would be
weeks more than months.

The rest of their words
fell softly on deaf ground.

I remembered in the morning
they had forecast an oncoming storm,

the tail end of a hurricane
from the Caribbean seas.

What do they know?
they never get things right,
it will never ever reach here.

I cried

They say big men don't cry. Well, I've cried streams and rivers that flowed into oceans. I cried when my first-born travelled across waters, resided deep in a sea palace for nine months before entering into my world. Years later I cried when they had to cleave open the ripe melon womb to scoop out the heart of flesh and redness that was my second child. When my daughter made her appearance I cried and she hollered and I told her I'd never let her go. I cried when I saw my wife coming down the aisle and I told her I'd love her forever, the same tears that turned into anger and frustrations at the different roads we took and all that we had, had turned into a crumbling tower of Babel. I cried at the words we threw at each other, the land mines we walked upon and the bitter barbed wire that wrapped around both of us. I cried when France won the World Cup a multi-cultural team breaking walls of indifference, but the police put the walls back up and the people rioted, because another black man was shot on the streets of Paris. I cried at a tangerine coloured sunset that I'll never see again and moons so large that they fill lakes to overflowing. I've cried during the playing of Anita Baker or was it the intense sweet loving of you, the way you cry when I place my mouth on you, devouring the rich, moist, honeyed centre of you and the secrets that open like a bright pink rose. Oh, I cry with a passion when I enter you, rise in you, travel the length of this universe within you, rivers that pour into you and over you. I've loved angels without wings who sing their hearts filled with love songs making me cry in the spring time, only to watch love fall like autumn leaves.

I'm crying right now watching my mum holding on, each cough, each grunt, watching her getting ready to fly her maiden flight from my world into her paradise. They say big men don't cry but I'm crying streams and rivers that are flowing into oceans.

The map of your leg

In hospital your legs are unusually dry
after a weekend lying in bed, it's
the third time in a month
you've been brought here,
same ward, same nurses,
same uncertainty, this time
you can't move your right leg.
It's autumn outside and the leaves
are falling, crispy golden brown,
curled, begging for moisture.
You're unable to rub the cream
in your own skin so I begin.
There's a survey of marks across your legs
mapping time and continents,
the basin of scar on your shin bone
that carries you back to the teenager
daring to backchat your mother.
You remember so clearly
the fire wood thrown at you
that catches you, sticks out of your leg,
a gush flowing from an open wound.
As I cream your ankle I find
there's a knot of scars,
at the side of your foot.
You're a child climbing trees
who loves the danger of it all,
until you fall, piercing the side of your foot.
The map of your leg draws me to the
blemishes of darkness

contrasted against the veneer of
your hazel-coloured skin, tint of ochre.
Silky smooth and beautiful
once again, as it should be,
your smile turns down
and you ask me
What have they done to me?
The chemotherapy? The radiation?
they've told me that these are the signs
of the cancer returning again.
I continue creaming your skin
but I can't tell you yet.

The first time

My mother's struggling to breathe,
gasping, slapping her thighs.
We quickly grasp the mask
from an oxygen cylinder
she breathes and throws it away.
Her eyes are frantically wide
sweating desperation,
through every pore of her skin,
she calls on Jesus to take her home.
We call the ambulance.

Hiding

She's hiding things —
Last night, a fellow patient
wandered the wards
calling to past memories and
harassing those of the present;

She waved her stick at mother
and told her to get out.
My mother laughed at her
and told her to go to bed.
We found out much, much later.

She hides food and gifts,
not to upset visitors and staff
and then gives me bags full to take away.

She's hiding the pain
that lines her face
as she greets everybody with her warm embrace.

She hides her anger over
family quarrels
and the way we behave toward each other.

She's hiding the knowing
of her ending
wrapped in smiles and avoidance.

She's hiding Bounty wrappers
for her sudden onslaught of
sweet guilty cravings.

She's hiding things that she finds,
folding tissues filled with blood-stained sputum.

The Great Escape

Tunde

Last night my mother was curled up,
a foetus sitting up, back bent as
a crescent moon, I saw no light or sparkle
to ever imagine that she would go
missing in the light of day.

It was all a ruse, Tunde had a plan –
unplugged her from her oxygen
and with a drip of fluid and a wheelchair
they were gone, like Bonnie and Clyde.

Off the ward, along clinical corridors,
Tunde singing *I'll fly away*, telling
her about *Babylon and injustice
are like hand in glove*. He'll smile,
speak gentrified to the nurses and doctors
and when their backs are turned,
he'll slip into the lift and into his patois
*You see, Mother Mc, no one
can stop the redeemed* and I can see
you smiling, your body uncurling as
the elevator door opens,
and you feel the wind.
He can't take you outside yet,
the timing has to be right
so he detours to the canteen
slips you in the corner
quotes scripture and verse,
pulls out your favourite word-search

and like spies undercover
you break the code of life
waiting for the right combination
to make your great getaway.

Tunde takes you back
to Daddy Mc where you're
walking side by side to church.
The yearly trips to Brighton.
Tunde brings out the coup de grace –
a flask of Saturday soup.
The wisp alone causes you
to straighten your back
and you only take a few
mouthfuls but you're getting ready,
and Tunde sees it too
so he wraps the blanket around you
and he makes for the door
the light pours on you, your
face glows a golden brown
and you're seeing things.
The trees stretch their branches
and the wind sounds like
a choir of angels and you hear
a familiar voice, a voice you
long to be with.
Birds sing a new song, as though
Mother Nature was saying you're
nearly there, and you're
standing tall, your spirit
alive ready to fly…

One last Psalm before you go to sleep

I'm not feeling God like I used to –
not with the same blind devotion,
not like the seven-year-old you taught
to read a Psalm before I go to sleep.

A Psalm to manage anger
A Psalm to deliver us from danger
A Psalm for the ones who let us down
A Psalm of healing for broken hearts and broken homes.

So I grab the late night embers
of a burning belief that you set alight in me
and read the Psalms with a glowing urgency
as if someone had breathed upon me.

A Psalm for the sun rise
A Psalm for the sunset
A Psalm to shine in the darkest hour of midnight
A Psalm that trails its glory across the firmaments.

There's one last twinkle in your eye
a tightness in your grip and I realise
I've never stopped reading, never stopped holding.
You were the loving Psalms in my life, day and night

and…
        The Psalms that becomes I
                        and I become the Psalms
that lies next to you before you go to sleep.

Beginning with your last breath

If poetry could take the pain away
it would begin with your last breath;
capture it, re-write, re-verse your life.
I'd be holding you close to my chest
like an accordion watching the bellows
of your lungs being pushed and pressed
to hear one last sweet melody.
I would uncurl your worn-out body,
withdraw all needles, catheters and appendages,
return a half-cut lung, replace a chopped bowel,
send concoctions of pills back to the source,
and spots and shadows on MRI scans
would no longer haunt you.

If poetry could take the pain away
you'd be back opening the front door,
to safe havens where love grew and harmony
was sewn into the very fabric of your home.
You'd be sitting in your living room
singing the *Old Rugged Cross*
with Jimmy Swaggart on the God Channel until
it was time to switch over to your evening soap.
You'd be like a wind chime playing in the wind
as we all breezed in, sons and daughters,
grandchildren and friends watching you
in the kitchen preparing meals seasoned with peace
and a smile to disarm any family quarrel.

If poetry could take the pain away
I'd swap places and it would be me
struggling to breathe

that five-year-old child you held close
to your bosom like a small bagpipe
limped limbs, lungs bulging,
inflating and deflating;
to capture,
to write,

to verse my life
to begin with my first breath
with you watching over me
until the break of dawn.

Nearly There (II)

You remember the time I was caught in a snowstorm
coming from school, cutting through the fields behind us,
a winter wonderland turned into a white nightmare
of knee deep snow with a horizontal blizzard
blowing into a young teenager making his way home.

Bruised benumbed by a bombardment of snow
bent doubled like a soldier, I begged
for the siege to end, sobbed as I struggled,
cried your name as I stiffened
in the numbing coldness of the air.

But I could hear you telling me to keep going on

The snow-slates, so large, so sharp,
felt like being stoned to submission,
weighed down, held down, I'm praying
with my head bowed down, body beaten cold.
I'm near home, nearing the corner of my road.

And I hear you telling me to keep going on.

And you're there waiting for me, door open
drawing me in from the cold. Shovelling snow
from my frozen body, you place me by the coal fire
and bring me a bowl of cornmeal porridge
and wrap yourself around me.
I'm still in the throes of winter.

But I hear you telling me to keep going on.

Notes

'A Soldier's Arabic' by Brian Turner from *Here, Bullet* (Bloodaxe Books, 2007).

'Twelve Notes for A Light Song of Light' by Kei Miller from *A Light Song of Light* (Carcanet Press, 2010).

That place just off the M6
Yam, yam colloquial for local Black Country people. *Nyam* Jamaican patois to eat. *Yam* starchy dry plant, boiled and roasted, native to the Africa diaspora.

The *black corner* of Wolverhampton
Blakenhall – *the Old English blæc', meaning 'black' or dark coloured, & 'halh' meaning 'nook' or 'corner'* – Wikipedia

Patterson's House
'Beulah' has also been used in literature as the name of a mystical place, somewhere between Earth and Heaven. It was so used in *The Pilgrim's Progress* by John Bunyan and in the works of William Blake – Wikipedia.

Tebbit Test
Lord Tebbit of the Conservative party once suggested the controversial *'cricket test'* in which the loyalty of British Blacks and Asians could be measured by who they supported in international cricket matches.

Burning with rage…
Torch of hate was an inflammatory headline in *The Star* newspaper blazened on the front page with a picture of a black young man with a further headline *face of a bomber*.

Bring me my Bow of burning gold;
Bring me my Arrows of desire:
Bring me my Spear: O clouds unfold!
Bring me my Chariot of fire!

This verse from 'Jerusalem' by William Blake was taken from preface to his epic *Milton: A Poem*.

Finding *X-Self*

This poem contains the lines *'towards / My heart at wounded knee'* and *'towards / Red Tacky bleeding in the West'* quoted from *X/Self* by Edward Kamau Brathwaite (Oxford University Press, 1987).

Never say goodbye

Never say goodbye is the translation of Kabhi Alvida Naa Kehna, a famous Indian musical romantic drama starring Shah Rukh Khan.

Tipton

Oss horse; *saft* foolish; *cut* canal; *ond* hand.*Pie Factory* famous pub and eatery. *Tipton Slasher* famous Tipton bareknuckle boxer. *Anchor* a monument to the chain industry. The Black Country *Living museum*.

I cried

In mid-December 1998, there were riots in immigrant neighbourhoods in the southwestern city of Toulouse, sparked when a policeman shot dead a 17-year old youth of Algerian origin during a car theft (Migration News: Jan 1999, Volume 6, Number 1)

Acknowledgements

I'd like to thank the Forward Prize for highly commending 'Papers' for the Poetry Prize; published in the *Forward Book of Poetry 2017*. I'd like to thank the following for the temporary home given to many of my poems that have appeared, sometimes in different versions; *Under the Radar, The Reader, The Cannon's Mouth* and *The Undertow Review*. Anthologies; *Out of Bounds* (Bloodaxe 2012) and *Celebrate Wha* (Smokestack 2011).

I want to thank *Love in Leamington* for Love Supreme and the musical collaboration with Steve Tromans and Lydia Glanville. And finally give thanks to Bohdan Piasecki and Apples & Snakes for bringing the life story of Bevan (who appears in many of the poems) to the Birmingham MAC.

I'm indebted to everyone who helped me along the way with this collection including all my family and friends; to Paul Grant, Phillip Simpson and Predencia my inner circle; the Warwick Write Sparks Collective for providing a space for growth; and Writers Without Borders for the spirit and love provided in the quiet times.

Special thanks for Jane Commane for her grace, insight and friendship and to Maish for your love and just being there.